AF342370

A PROJECT GUIDE TO

FISH & AMPHIBIANS

Carol Parenzan Smalley

A Project Guide to:
Exploring Earth's Biomes • **Fish and Amphibians** •
Mammals • Projects in Genetics • Reptiles and Birds •
Sponges, Worms, and Mollusks

PUBLISHER'S NOTE: The facts on which the story
in this book is based have been thoroughly
researched. Documentation of such research
can be found on page 44. While every possible
effort has been made to ensure accuracy, the
publisher will not assume liability for damages
caused by inaccuracies in the data, and
makes no warranty on the accuracy of the
information contained herein. The Internet
sites referenced herein were active as of the
publication date. Due to the fleeting nature of
some web sites, we cannot guarantee they will
all be active when you are reading this book.

Library of Congress
Cataloging-in-Publication Data

Smalley, Carol Parenzan, 1960–
 A project guide to fish and amphibians /
Carol Parenzan Smalley.
     p. cm. — (Life science projects for kids)
 Includes bibliographical references and
index.
  ISBN 978-1-58415-873-8 (library bound)
 1. Fishes—Experiments—Juvenile literature.
 2. Amphibians—Experiments—Juvenile
literature. I. Title.
  QL618.5.S63 2011
  597.078—dc22
                                              2010030900

Printing   1   2   3   4   5   6   7   8   9

                                              PLB

CONTENTS

INTRODUCTION

Humans, **fish**, and **amphibians** have something in common. They are **vertebrates**, or animals with backbones. Like those of flounder and frogs, human backbones are internal, which means they lie within the body structure.

But fish and amphibians are also different than humans. Both are **ectothermic**, or cold blooded. Their body temperature goes higher or lower depending on the temperature of the environment. Humans, like other **mammals**, are **endotherms**, or warm blooded, and our body temperature usually remains the same.

Most amphibians and fish reproduce by laying eggs. However, there are some fish, such as the shark, that are **viviparous**, which means the fish develops inside its mother before being born live. Humans are also viviparous.

Both fish and amphibians begin their lives in an aquatic environment, but only fish remain there. An amphibian moves from water to land, either partially or completely. (The word *amphibian* comes from two Greek words, *amphi* and *bios,* meaning "two lives.")

Amphibians include frogs and toads; salamanders, newts, and **sirens**; and **caecilians** (limbless amphibians that resemble worms). They have no skin covering, such as feathers or scales. As adults, they breathe using lungs. Sometimes, they also breathe through their skin.

There are more than 25,000 different types of fish.[1] They include jawless fish, **cartilaginous** fish, and bony fish. Fish live in water, have scales, use gills to breathe, and use fins to move. They can live in either saltwater (oceans) or freshwater (rivers and lakes). Some fish, such as salmon, are **anadromous**. They are born in freshwater, migrate to saltwater to live, and return to freshwater to reproduce.

Some scientists believe that amphibians evolved from fish. These scientists believe that during the **Devonian** period, **crossopterygians**, a type of lobe-finned fish, left water for land and became the first amphibians.[2] Other scientists are exploring a new discovery buried deep in Pennsylvania rock, which they believe shows a preserved timeline of life development on Earth. They think they have found a link between fish and animals that walk on land, including humans.[3]

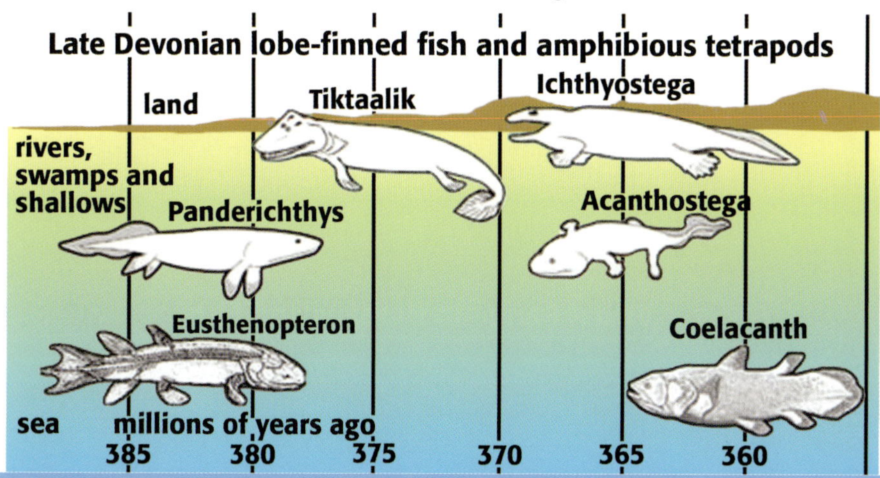

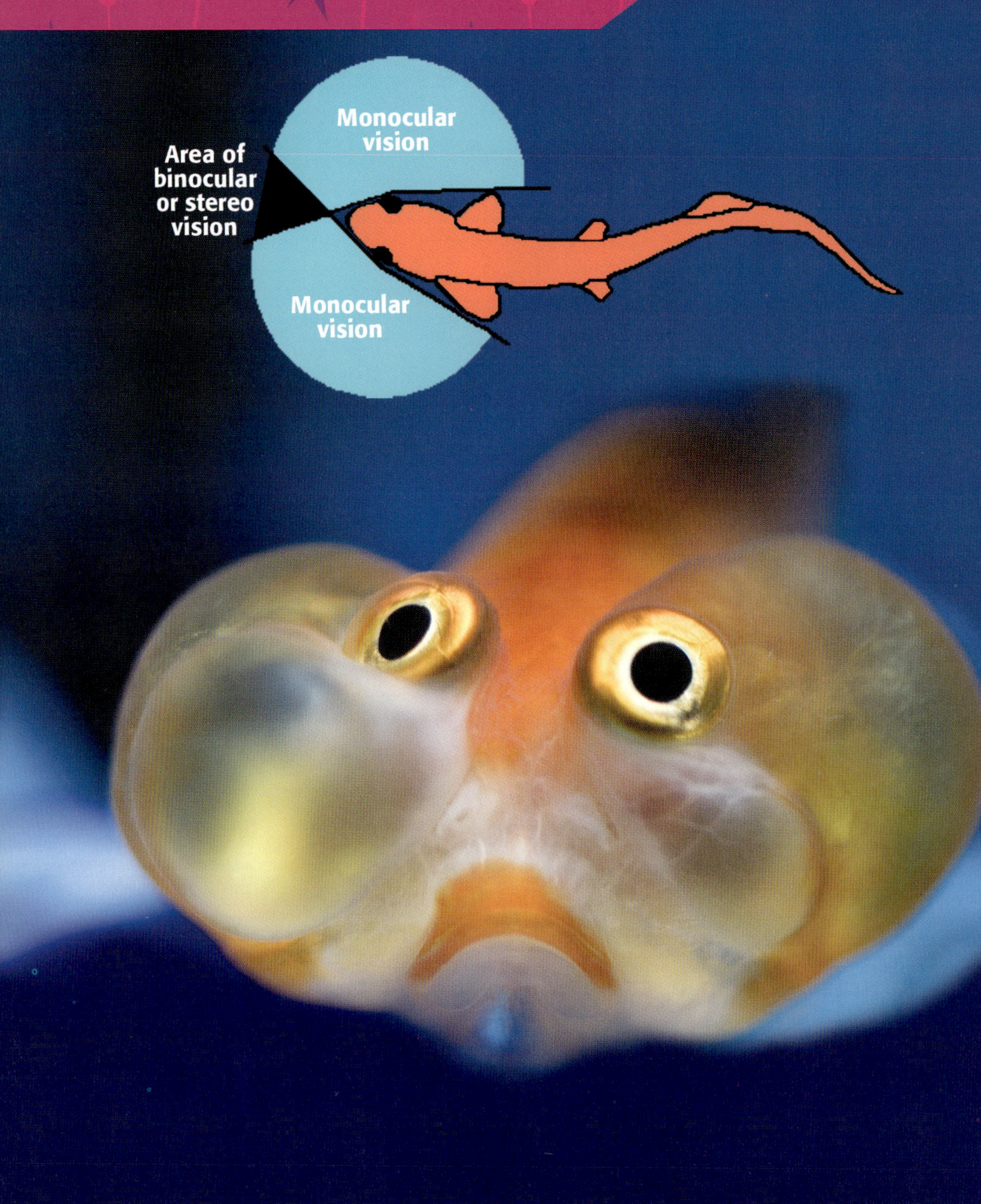

Visual Range in Humans and Fish

Entity	Horizontal	Vertical	Binocular
Human	154°	150°	25°
Fish	165°	134°	12°

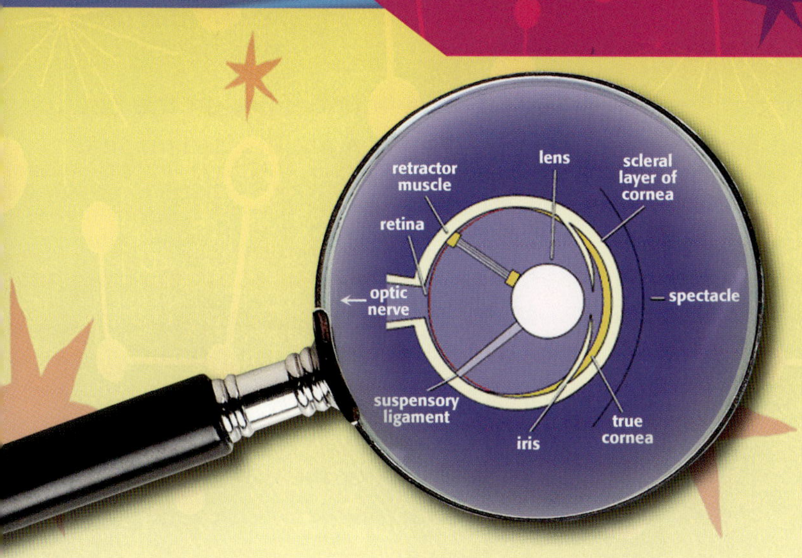

FISH EYES

Fish see images differently than humans do. The two eyes on a human's face work together to allow for **binocular vision**. The word *binocular* comes from two Latin roots: *bini* for "double" and *oculus* for "eye."[1] When both eyes are open, your eyes look at objects from a slightly different angle from each other. They allow you to see an object and determine the distance the object is from you. This ability is called **depth perception**.

Fish, however, have **monocular vision**. (*Monocular* means "one eye.") They don't have only one eye, but in monocular vision, each eye works independently of the other. With monocular vision, the field of vision is increased. Fish can see and track two different objects at the same time, which helps them see more of their environment at once. The left eye can focus on one image. The right eye can focus on another. Because the two eyes work independently, fish have limited depth perception.

Flatfish, such as flounder, are an interesting exception. A flounder **larva** has one eye on each side of its head. However, as it changes from its juvenile form to its adult form, one of the eyes moves across the face and joins the other. An adult flounder has both eyes on one side

of its head. To protect itself from predators, a flounder lies on the bottom of the ocean floor with its "blind side" down and its "seeing side" up.

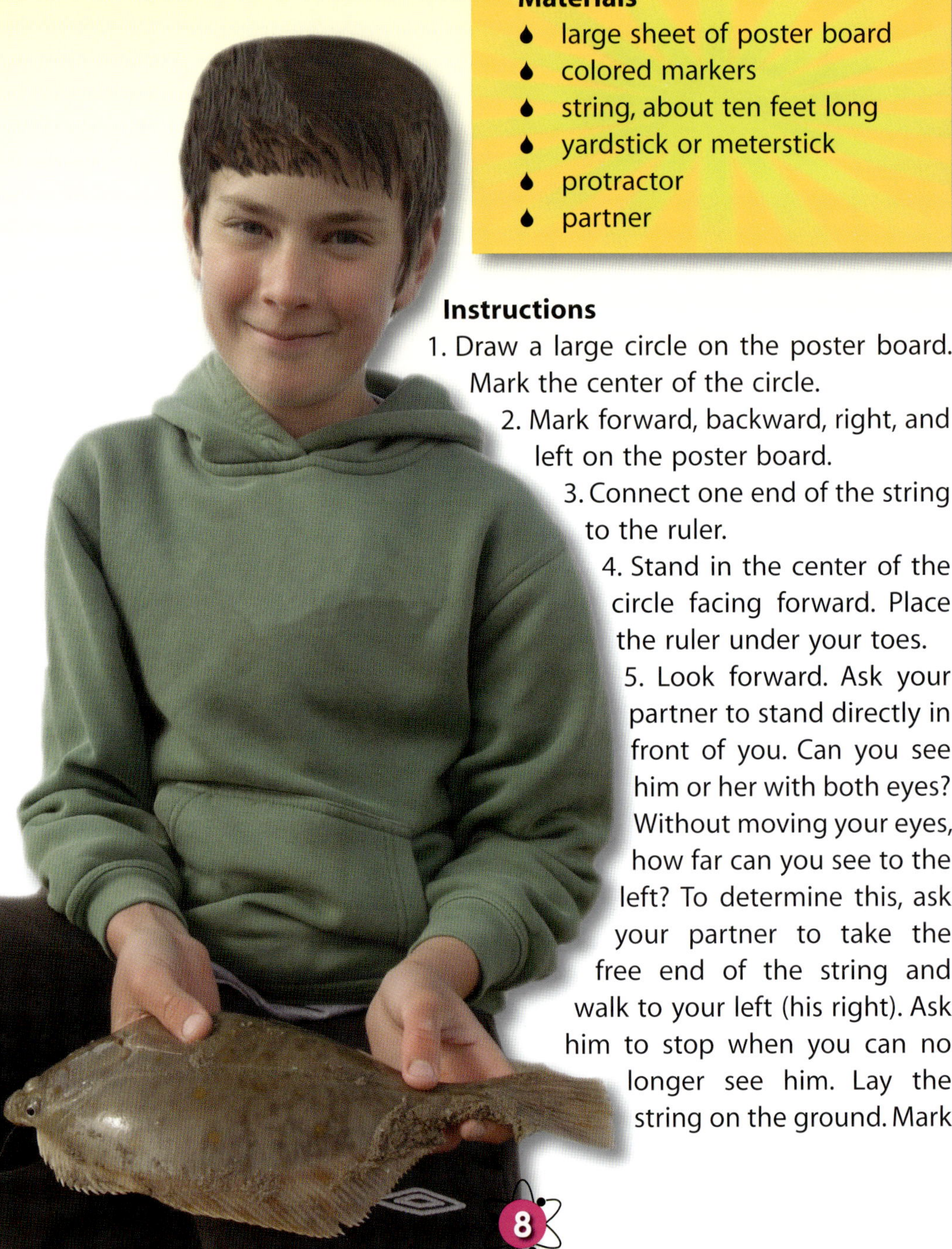

Materials
- large sheet of poster board
- colored markers
- string, about ten feet long
- yardstick or meterstick
- protractor
- partner

Instructions
1. Draw a large circle on the poster board. Mark the center of the circle.
2. Mark forward, backward, right, and left on the poster board.
3. Connect one end of the string to the ruler.
4. Stand in the center of the circle facing forward. Place the ruler under your toes.
5. Look forward. Ask your partner to stand directly in front of you. Can you see him or her with both eyes? Without moving your eyes, how far can you see to the left? To determine this, ask your partner to take the free end of the string and walk to your left (his right). Ask him to stop when you can no longer see him. Lay the string on the ground. Mark

on the circle the location where the string intersects the circle. Label this as "both eyes—binocular vision left."

6. How far can you see to the right? Repeat the same sequence as in step 5, but this time, have your partner move to your right, or his left. Do not move your eyes. Label this as "both eyes—binocular vision right."

7. Draw a line from each of the two points on the circle to the center of the circle. Using your protractor, determine your binocular field of vision for both eyes.

8. Stand in the center of the circle again. Cover your right eye. Ask your partner to move first to your left/his right. Do not move your eyes. Have him stop when you can no longer see him. Using a different color marker, note this location on the circle. Then, ask him to move to your right/his left. Again, have him stop when you can no longer see him. Note this location. Label this as "left eye only—monocular vision."

9. Repeat step 8 with your other eye. Do not move your eyes. Using a different color, label this as "right eye only—monocular vision."

10. Connect the points you just found to the center of the circle, and measure the angles with your protractor.

11. The area of overlap for steps 8 and 9 is where you have depth perception. Show this with another color.

12. With your body facing forward, turn your head to the right so that your nose is directly over your right shoulder. (This simulates a fish seeing out of one eye only.) Cover your left eye. Allowing your eyes (and not your head) to move, with your partner helping you, determine how far you can see to the left and to the right using the same process as before. Using a different color, label this "monocular vision—right eye."

13. Repeat on the left side. With a different color, label this "monocular vision—left eye."

14. How far can you see around you with monocular vision? Are there any blind spots?

15. Which type of vision do you think is better? Why?

FISH DRAFTING

Olympic swimming champion Michael Phelps has learned from schools of fish in the ocean. They taught him how to draft.

Envision a boat moving through the water. The V that forms behind the boat is its draft. Water in the V moves toward the boat to replenish the water that was displaced when the boat cut through the water.

As a boat, swimmer, or fish propels through the water, its energy is transferred to the water behind it. Another boat, swimmer, or fish behind the first one can use that energy to move forward.

In the pool, a slower swimmer may draft a faster swimmer by hanging close on his heels. Although this can be somewhat annoying to the lead swimmer, the second swimmer is actually using the energy in the lead swimmer's wake, or water movement, to propel himself forward.

Fish do the same thing. They use each other's energy to conserve their own.

Materials
- a group of 5 to 10 friends
- **an adult** or lifeguard to supervise
- a shallow (waist-deep) swimming pool,
  or use the shallow end of a pool at a community center

Instructions

1. Run randomly through the water for about two minutes. Do not follow a pattern. Allow each "fish" to chart his or her own course. Go forward, to the left, to the right; reverse direction quickly. How much energy did this require?

2. Select one runner to be the lead fish. All other fish must follow the leader in his or her path. Do not pass. Do not get out of line. After 30 seconds, have the leader drop from the lead and go to the end of the "school." Continue for another 30 seconds. Again, change positions. Do this until everyone has had a turn being the leader. In which position was the most energy required? In which position was the least energy required? Why?

3. Form a circle with everyone's left shoulder toward the inside of the circle. Run in a circle for 30 seconds. Quickly, reverse direction. Run with everyone's right shoulder toward the inside of the circle for 30 seconds. Quickly, reverse direction. Run for 30 seconds. Quickly, lift your feet off the bottom of the pool and float. What do you discover?

4. How can you relate this experience to that of a school of fish?

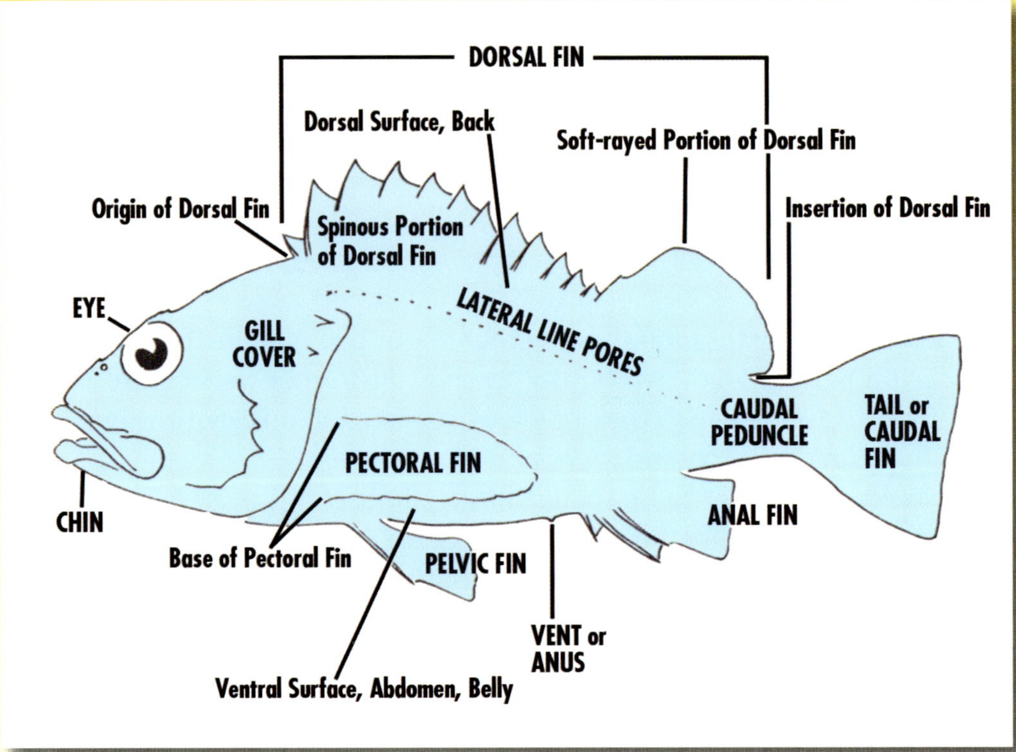

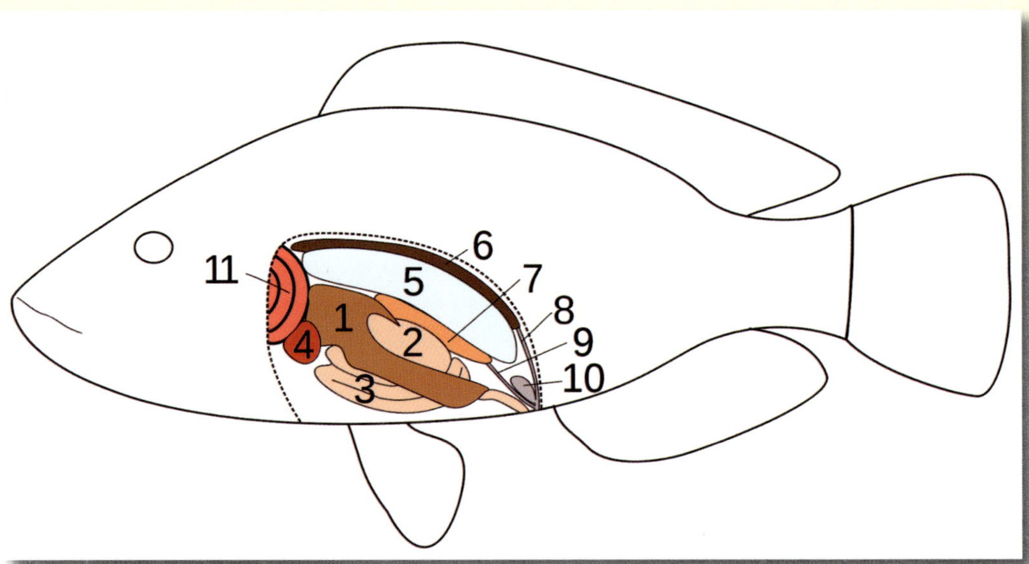

Inner anatomy of a fish: 1. liver, 2. stomach, 3. intestine, 4. heart, 5. swim bladder, 6. kidney, 7. testicle, 8. ureter, 9. efferent duct, 10. urinary bladder, 11. gills

FISH FLOATS

To swim, fish move their tail and fins. Their skin or scales (and a covering of mucus on some fish) help them glide smoothly through the water. Most fish also have a swim bladder that lets them stay at different depths of water.

Different types of fish have different combinations of fins. The tail is actually a fin called a caudal fin. On the back is the dorsal fin, on the belly is the ventral fin, and on the sides are pectoral fins.

The swim bladder is a balloon-like organ inside many types of fish. The fish fills or empties the swim bladder depending on whether it wants to go up, down, or stay at the same depth. It uses mostly oxygen and nitrogen from the water to make it more buoyant, which makes it rise in the water. When it wants to go down, it releases the gases from the swim bladder.

To see how a fish maintains buoyancy, try this experiment.

Materials
- clear plastic container, at least 10 inches deep
- water
- empty water or soda bottle, with lid
- 5 balloons
- marker

1. Fill a clear plastic container halfway with water.
2. Put an empty water or soda bottle, with its lid on tight, in

the container. Does the bottle sink or float? Try pushing the bottle to the bottom of the container. What happens when you let go?

3. Half fill the bottle with water and replace the cap. Put the bottle back in the container. Does it sink or float? Push the bottle to the bottom of the container. What happens when you let it go?

4. Fill the water bottle completely and replace the cap. Does it sink or float now? Try to make it float. What happens?

5. You can try the same type of experiment using balloons. Fill the balloons with different amounts of air and water. Label the balloons: air (full); water (full); half air and half water; 2/3 air and 1/3 water; 1/3 air and 2/3 water.

6. Place all the balloons in the container of water. Which ones sink? Which ones float? Which ones stay suspended in the water? Do some sink farther than others?

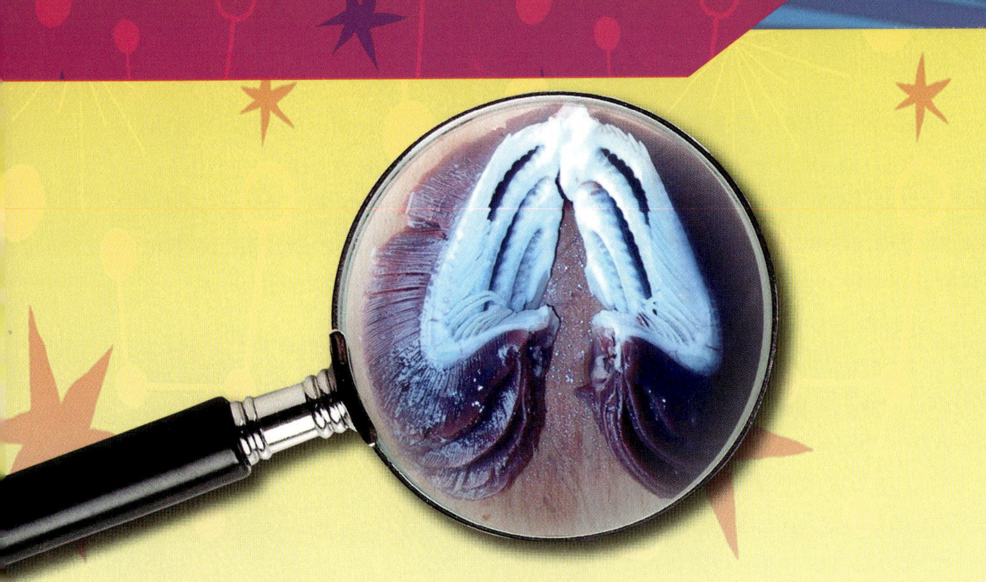

RESPIRATION RATES

Fish use gills to breathe, and, during the aquatic part of their lives, so do amphibians. Gills filter oxygen and other important gases from the water. From the gills, these gases enter the bloodstream.

Because they are cold-blooded, fish and amphibians take on the temperature of their surroundings. If the temperature changes too much, they move to deeper or shallower water, or they slow down their **metabolism** to conserve energy. When they do this, their breathing slows down, too. Each time a fish breathes, its gill covers open and close.

Test how a fish reacts to different water temperatures by warming and cooling the water in which it lives. (Don't worry. This will not harm the fish.) You can count the number of times a fish breathes by watching its gills.

Materials

- fish, such as a goldfish
- fish tank
- thermometer
- stopwatch or clock with second hand
- clear jar or fishbowl large enough to hold the fish and plenty of water
- net
- sunny window
- ice cubes
- pen
- graph paper

Instructions

1. Record the temperature of the water in a fish tank. Watch one of the fish in the tank to find out how many times it breathes in

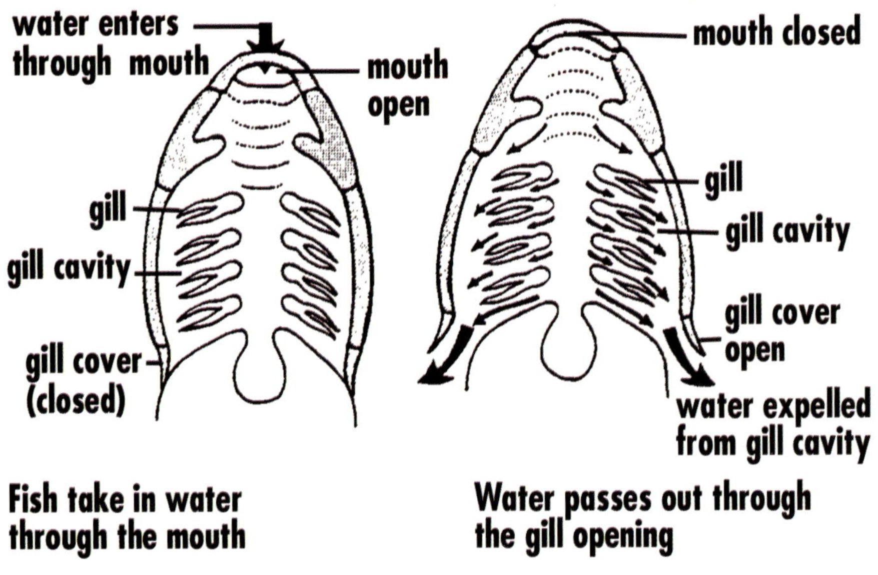

fifteen seconds. Multiply that number by 4 to find the number of breaths it takes in one minute. Record the data in a notebook.

2. Using the net, carefully transfer the fish to a jar or fishbowl filled with water from the tank. Be sure the jar is large enough for the fish to move easily and have water to breathe. Place the thermometer in the jar, and put the jar on a sunny windowsill. When the temperature starts to rise, record the new temperature and the respiration rate of the fish. Also note how the fish behaves. Continue taking measurements and recording the fish's behavior until you have two or three more sets of data. Do not let the water temperature change by more than 10°F (5°C).

3. As soon as you have your data, return the fish and the water to the tank and let the fish rest.

4. Repeat step 1.

5. Add ice cubes to the tank to gradually cool the water. Record new temperatures and respiration rates until you have three additional sets of data. Also record the behavior of the fish. Do not let the water temperature change by more than 10°F (5°C).

6. Using graph paper, graph your data, showing the relationship between temperature and breathing rates. What can you conclude from your graph?

SCALE TALES

Not all fish have scales. Some fish have no protective layer at all. Fish biologists call them naked fish. Other fish, such as the pinecone and pineapple fish, are covered in bony growths called scutes.[1]

Most fish, however, have one of four types of scales to protect them:

- **Placoid** scales are similar to teeth. They are shaped like thorns and, like teeth, are composed of dentin and covered by protective enamel. A shark has placoid scales.
- **Ganoid** scales are flat and rhombus-shaped. They may or may not overlap. Ganoid scales can be found on gars.
- **Cycloid** scales are small round or oval scales, often showing growth rings. Salmon have cycloid scales.
- **Ctenoid** scales have spines on one edge of the scale. They may also show growth rings. Halibut have this type of scales.[2]

On some fish, the scales show a lateral line—a line that runs down each side of the fish from the gills to the tail. This organ allows the fish to feel vibrations in the water. This ability helps them avoid obstacles in the water and to find prey. Electric eels and some other fish have a modified lateral line that allows them to feel electrical impulses in the water, including magnetic fields. Scientists believe that fish use this organ, along with the ampullae of Lorenzini, to detect Earth's magnetic

The ampullae of Lorenzini are clusters of jelly-filled pores that detect electrical impulses in the water. Tiny hairs around the pores vibrate, sending a signal to a nerve in the pore. Sharks and rays have very sensitive ampullae of Lorenzini.

field. This helps them stay on course when they migrate long distances. Since animals produce an electrical field when they move their muscles, these organs also help them locate prey.

You can see how fish detect vibrations in the water by doing the following experiment.

Materials
- gelatin, such as Jell-O brand (any flavor)
- mixing bowl
- spoon
- stove
- **an adult**
- Styrofoam bowls
- refrigerator
- toothpicks

Instructions
1. With **an adult** to help you, follow the directions on the packet to make gelatin.
2. Pour the gelatin into small Styrofoam bowls. Refrigerate until the gelatin is firm.
3. Poke a hole into the side of one of the bowls with a toothpick. Push the toothpick into the gelatin, but leave part of it sticking out of the bowl.
4. Insert a second toothpick into the top of the gelatin, but leave part of the toothpick sticking out of the top.
5. Tap the gelatin near the top toothpick. What happens? What happens when you wiggle the top toothpick?

The toothpick on the top detects the "electrical signals" in the water. The toothpick at the side represents the nerve, which sends the signal to the fish.

WHILE THE FISH WAS SWIMMING

History swims slowly at Chicago's Shedd Aquarium, home to Granddad, a lungfish that is at least 80 years old. The 25-pound, four-foot-long Australian fish arrived in Chicago in 1933 for the World's Fair. At the time, the fish was unusual. It breathed with both gills and lungs. The veterinarians at the aquarium can only guess as to its real age.[1] They believe it is the oldest living fish in captivity in the world. Some wild fish live more than 100 years.

One way to determine the age of a deceased fish is to examine its bones. Like trees, bones have growth rings. **Ichthyologists** (fish scientists) study growth rings on vertebrae, scales, and **otoliths** (ear bones). They examine two types of rings: wide dark rings and thin see-through rings. They believe that the wide rings form in the summer, during quicker growth, and the thin rings form in the winter, during slower growth. Together, the two rings represent one year's growth. By counting pairs of rings, scientists can determine the animal's age.

Granddad

Materials
- computer with Internet access
- printer
- colored pencils

Instructions
1. Do an Internet image search for the term *otolith*.
2. Select a cross-section otolith image that clearly shows growth rings. The more rings the better! Print the otolith image.
3. Using two or more different colored pencils, color each ring set.
4. Count the ring sets to determine the fish's age.

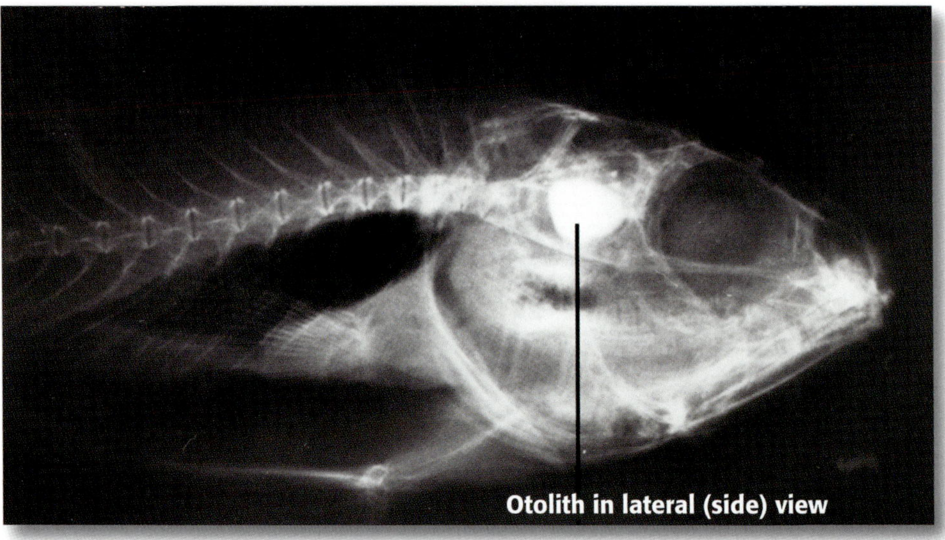

Otolith in lateral (side) view

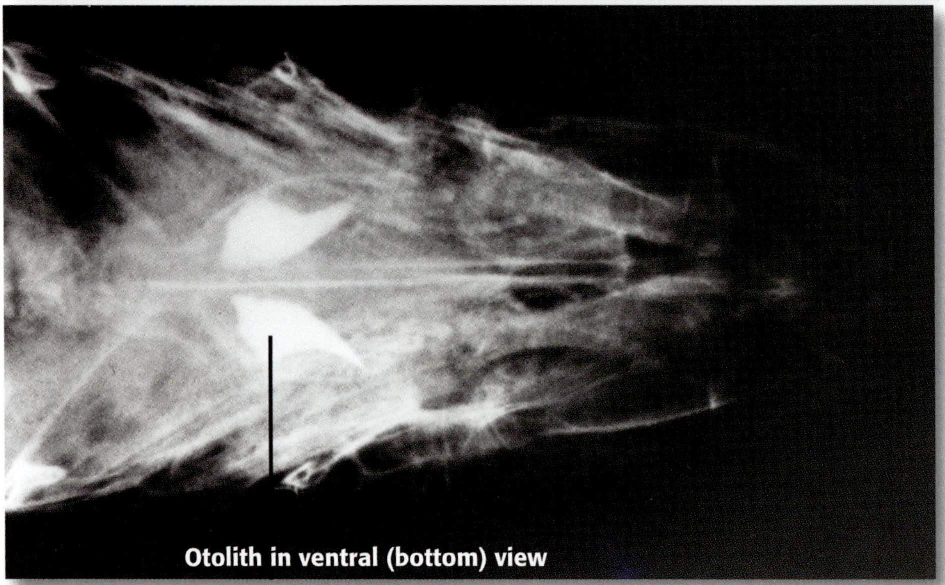

Otolith in ventral (bottom) view

5. For the purpose of this project, assume the fish died during the current calendar year. With the outermost ring representing this year, label each ring and the year the growth would have occurred. Work from the outermost ring to the center.

6. Pair the dates of each year of bone growth to significant events in your life, your family's history, or important events in the history of your school or community.

CROAKIN' COMMUNICATIONS

Frogs croak to communicate. They also trill and sing distinct patterns on key.

Peter M. Narins is a scientist who studies animals and their communication patterns. He studied the male coqui frog, which makes two sounds—a *co* and a *qui* (KEE). Large male frogs sound out once every four seconds. Smaller coquis *co* and *qui* once every two seconds. Rarely do competing frogs' notes overlap. They sing from dusk till about midnight most nights, making music for their mates on the island of Puerto Rico.[1]

Another sound scientist, Robert R. Capranica, experimented with the communication responses

of a captive male bullfrog. When Capranica played an electronic version of another bullfrog's bellow, the captive frog responded. However, when he played **synthesized** calls from 34 other types of frogs and toads, the bullfrog remained silent, showing no response.[2]

Materials
- **an adult**
- a frog habitat at dusk
  (or a sound recording of frogs)
- staff paper (for musical notation)
- clipboard
- pencil
- something to sit on
- a flashlight
- bug repellent

Instructions

1. With **an adult**, visit a frog habitat at dusk. This could be a pond, wetland area, or nature preserve. (If you don't have an area to visit, borrow a nature recording from your library.)

2. Using musical notation paper, record what you hear. If you know how to read and write music, be as accurate as possible. (You can find free, downloadable musical notation paper on the Internet.) If you don't know how to read and write music, make up your own notation.

   To help you, imagine a beat, or rhythm, in your head. Do the frogs communicate with every beat? Every other beat? Every third or fourth beat? Is there just one frog or more than one? Do they all make the same sound or different sounds? Do the sounds get louder or faster? Softer or slower?

   Do they appear to be communicating with each other?

3. With **an adult**, visit the same area on another night with different weather conditions. (It could be colder or overcast.) Record what you hear. How does this compare to the first recording?

HOW TO HEAR WITH NO (EXTERNAL) EARS

Humans have external ears to capture sound waves. The waves move the eardrum, and the vibrations are processed by the brain. Amphibians do not have external ears, but they still "hear" through vibrations.

Frogs have a membrane, or layer of skin, called a **tympanum** on either side of their head. Imagine a timpani drum, with its skin or head stretched tightly over the bowl. When struck, it vibrates. This is how a frog's membrane works as well. A frog's membrane vibrates according to sound waves.

Frogs also hear with their lungs.[1] These amphibians have a tube that connects their lungs to their eardrums. This tube allows vibrations felt within the frog's body to transfer to the frog's tympana for processing. These tubes also protect the frog's ear membrane.

Frogs can be quite vocal, often emitting calls exceeding 100 decibels—loud enough to damage human hearing. When the noise level reaches damaging levels, the sound can dissipate, or be reduced, through the ear tube.

Materials
- box of gelatin mix
- water
- refrigerator
- 1 quart (1 liter) circular bowl
- items that make a variety of sounds (high, low, short, long), such as voice, instruments, clapping hands, whistle, heavy book that you can drop, stereo or sound system
- paper and pencil
- a partner

Instructions
1. Prepare gelatin according to the package directions. Pour it into the bowl and allow the gelatin to set in the refrigerator. (Do not disturb the gelatin while it is setting. You want a smooth top layer.)
2. Place the prepared gelatin and bowl on a hard floor, such as wood or linoleum. (Do not place on carpet.)

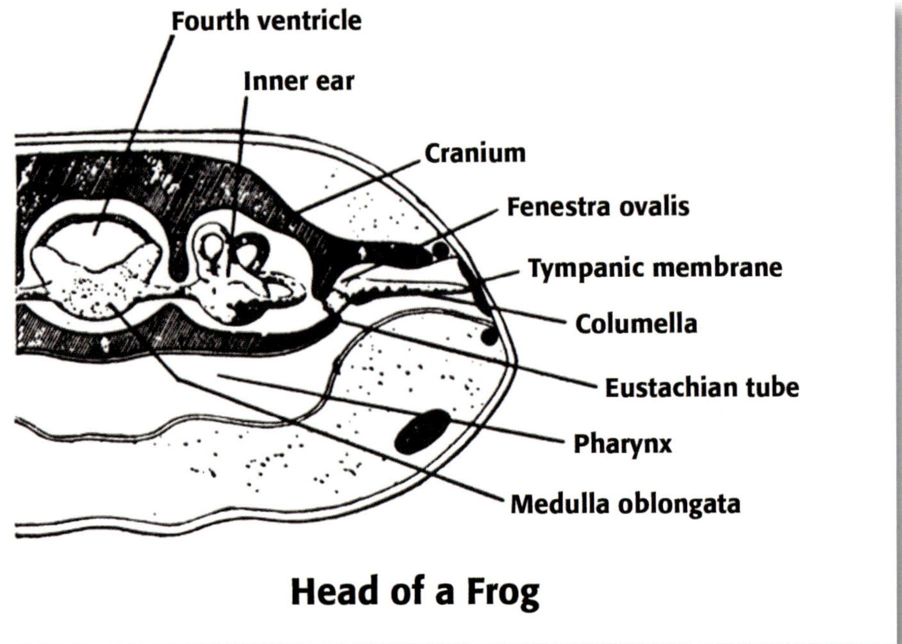

Head of a Frog

3. The gelatin represents the frog's tympanum. Make one sound at a time with your voice, instruments, etc., near the bowl. How does the gelatin respond to the various sounds?

Noise	Observed Effect

4. While you stay near the bowl to watch it, have another person walk across the floor. What do you notice?
5. Lie down on the hard floor and ask your partner to create a variety of sounds. Can you feel anything through the floor?
6. If you were a frog in the woods, how might you use your multiple methods of hearing for survival?

FROG GUTS

Have you ever heard an adult say: "When I went to school, I had to . . ."?

It wasn't that long ago when students were required to **dissect** animals as part of their science education. In 1988, 75 to 80 percent of all biology or life science students dissected frogs as part of their animal study.[1] The purpose was to observe the organs in an animal to see how they function.

Today, because of technology and the creation of virtual dissection labs, and because some students object to dissection, there are many alternative projects to learn the same material.

Numerous virtual dissection experiences are available on the Internet. (A free one is included in the Web resources on page 45.) Also, an online search for the words *frog anatomy* will provide many online resources of external and internal frog parts.

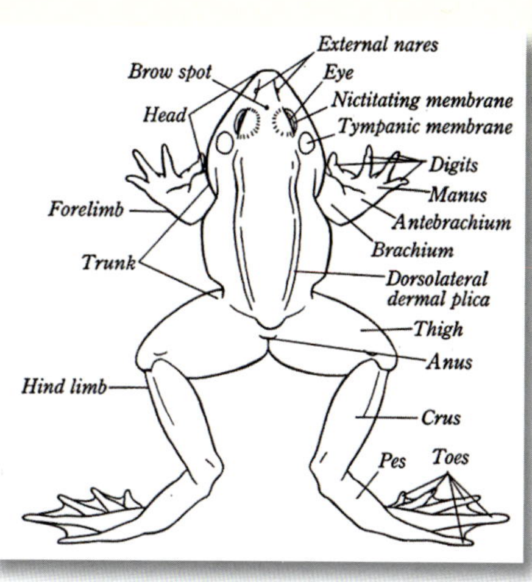

There is little need to cut into a frog to learn more about it. With just a click, you can study frogs and other animals online.

Materials
- roll of art paper, approximately 36 inches wide and about 6 feet long
- pencil
- a partner
- markers
- computer with Internet access

MODEL OF A FEMALE FROG'S ANATOMY

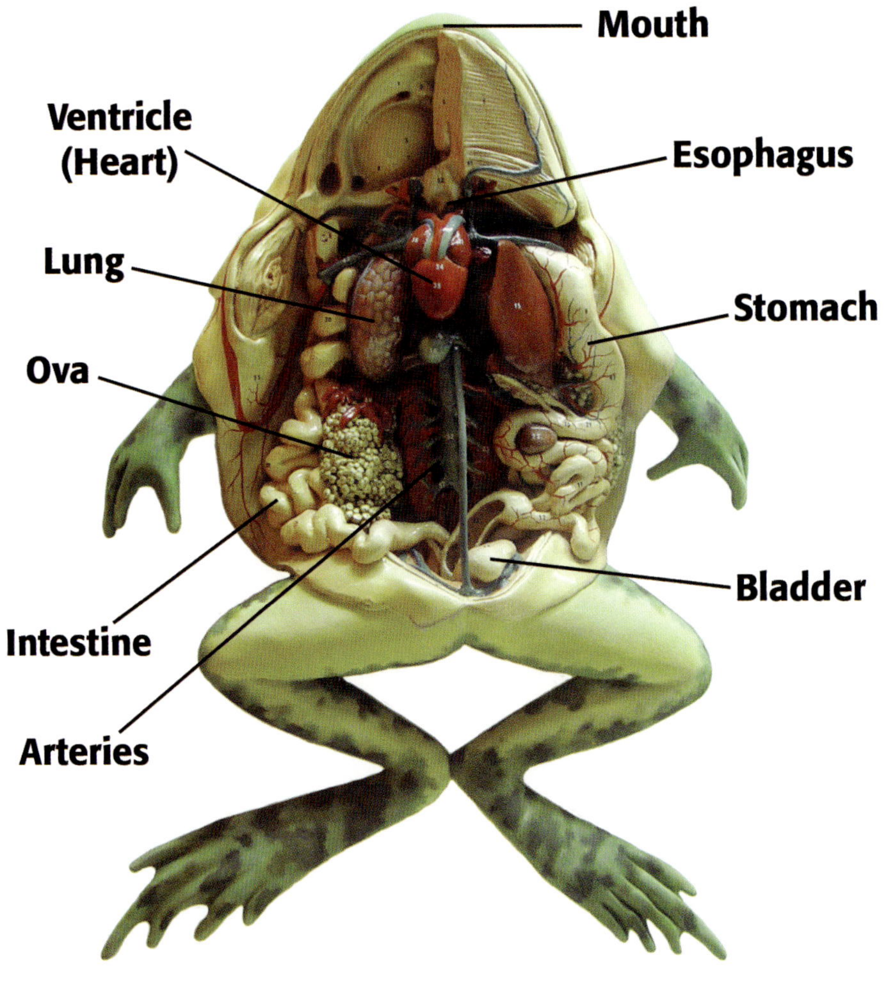

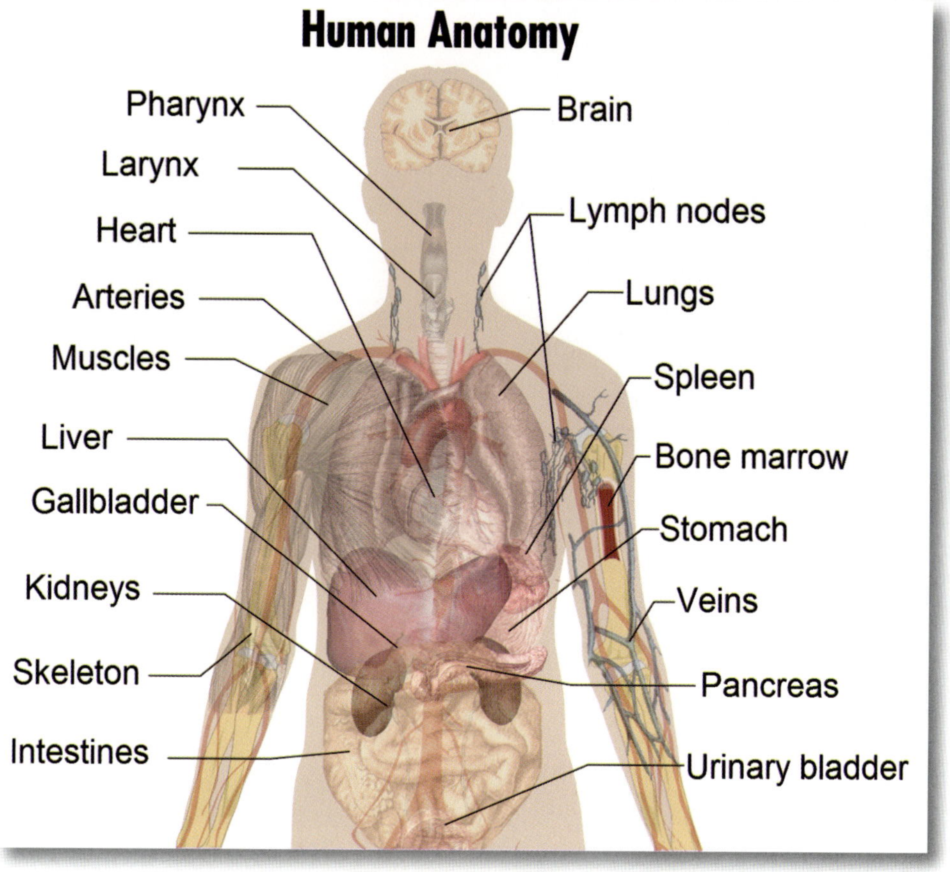
Human Anatomy
Pharynx
Larynx
Heart
Arteries
Muscles
Liver
Gallbladder
Kidneys
Skeleton
Intestines
Brain
Lymph nodes
Lungs
Spleen
Bone marrow
Stomach
Veins
Pancreas
Urinary bladder

Instructions

1. Lay a sheet of art paper on the floor.
2. Lie on your back on the paper. Have someone trace you.
3. Select and label at least ten external body parts (ear, hand, teeth, etc.) and at least ten internal body parts (stomach, lungs, specific bone, etc.). Add details to your tracing to show these body parts.
4. Using online and print resources to guide you, on the large sheet of paper, draw a frog to scale (in proportion to you) in the same position.
5. Find and label the corresponding body parts. Do you have body parts that frogs do not? Do frogs have body parts that you do not?

Like frogs and toads, amphibious salamanders go through several stages during their life cycle. When they hatch from eggs in water, they have feathery gills. Slowly, legs begin to grow. This is called the nymph stage. As they mature into adults, their gills begin to disappear and lungs develop. Some salamanders can live to be 20 years old.

SALAMANDER CROSSING

There is a strange traffic sign on Henry Street in Amherst, Massachusetts. It reads: Salamander Crossing.[1]

Every spring, migrating salamanders attempt to cross from one side of Henry Street to the other, where a pond awaits them. There, the salamanders mate and lay their eggs. In 1987, traffic engineers built two underground tunnels to help the salamanders cross safely.

Some salamanders are strictly **aquatic**—they spend their whole lives in water. Others are **terrestrial**—they are strictly land dwellers. And yet others are **amphibious**, living part of their lives in water and part on the land. Although salamanders are **nocturnal**, **naturalists** can spot them during daylight hours if they know where to look.

Spotted salamander eggs—Egg nucleus uncurls from center
Western slimy salamander
with hatchlings

Salamanders hide in dark, wet areas. They take shelter under felled trees and rocks. Sometimes they hide in woodpiles or under porches. Often, they are spotted in clearings following rain showers.

Materials
- **an adult**
- sketchbook or nature journal
- pencil or colored pencils
- clipboard
- flashlight
- sheet of cellophane
- rubber band
- amphibian nature guide or access to the Internet

Instructions

1. During daytime hours, under **adult** supervision, take a nature walk near a wetland, along a stream, or in the woods.
2. To look for salamanders, carefully lift logs and rocks. If you are near water, look in the water too, near the edge. They sometimes hide under rocks in ponds and creeks.
3. On your paper, record what you find, where you find it, and the time. Is it a single salamander or are they hiding in pairs or families? What do the salamanders look like? Are there special markings or stripes? How many toes? Make drawings to go with your notes.
4. With **an adult**, return to the same area just after dark. Using a flashlight covered with cellophane, look in open areas for salamanders. Check their hiding spots again. What do you see and where? Record your findings as you did earlier in the day.
5. Using your sketches and a nature guide, identify the salamanders.

NOTE: DO NOT remove any salamander from its natural habitat. DO NOT handle salamanders, as this will remove the protective coating from its skin. This coating allows the animal to breathe.

TOAD ABODE

During the drought of 2009, the piercing shrill of the endangered Houston toad of south-central Texas grew quiet. The amphibian's natural pond and marsh habitats were cracked and dry. Biologists estimated its wild population was once around 50,000 toads; they predicted that only 300 remained.[1] Those that survived the scorching summer heat buried themselves in mud or found shade.

Toads, like most amphibians, are sensitive to stresses in their environment. When exposed to toxic chemicals, including artificial fertilizers and **herbicides**, they can become ill or deformed. Sometimes, scientists study changes in amphibian populations to gauge the health of the animals' **ecosystem**.

Toads are a critical part of the ecosystems in which they live. A single toad can consume over 3,000 insects a month. As a nocturnal animal, the toad feasts primarily on slugs, worms, moths, and other invertebrates after dark.

Some gardeners like to attract toads to their vegetable and flower patches to control pest populations. Toads need four things to survive: food, water, a place to raise their offspring, and shelter. Nature has taken care of the food. A nearby pond or water garden will offer water.

A nontoxic environment is perfect for raising a toad family. And you can provide the shelter.

Materials
- clay flower pot, about six inches in diameter
- permanent markers
- a trowel (or large spoon)
- decaying leaves
- small flashlight
- nature journal
- pencil

Instructions:
1. Clean the pot thoroughly and let it dry.
2. With permanent markers, decorate the outside of your pot or toad house.
3. With the trowel, dig a hole about two to three inches deep.
4. Placing the pot on its side, bury one side of it so that half is above the ground.
5. Fill the pot with decaying leaves.
6. Check every day to see if the leaves are disturbed. If they are, a toad may have found its new home! (If after a few days a toad does not take up residence, move your home to another location.)
7. To observe the toad as it eats, position a flashlight in the soil to attract moths and other nighttime insects. Quietly observe and record the toad's dinner menu. How does the toad capture its dinner? What does it like to eat? What does it leave alone?

Introduction

1. Joseph S. Nelson. *Fishes of the World* (4th Edition). Hoboken, New Jersey: Wiley and Sons, 2006, pp. 4–5.

2. Armin Eskandari. "Evolution of Fish." PPT Presentation: http://www.authorstream.com/Presentation/eskandari2000-103231-evolution-fish-part-1-systematic-armin-eskandari-fish1-science-technology-ppt-powerpoint/ Hydrobiology Division, Biology Department, Faculty of Science HACETTEPE University , Beytepe Kampus, 06800, ANKARA, TURKEY.

3. "How Did Fins Evolve into Feet?" http://www.msnbc.msn.com/id/4638587/ns/technology_and_science-science/

Fish Eyes

1. Conway Livingstone, "Was Rembrandt Stereoblind?" *The New England Journal of* Medicine (Sep 2004) 351 (12): 1264–5. doi:10.1056/NEJM200409163511224.

2. E. A. Fairchild and W. H. Howell, "Factors Affecting the Post-release Survival of Cultured Juvenile *Pseudopleuronectes americanus*." *Journal of Fish Biology*. 65 (Supplementary A): 69-87. http://cinemar.unh.edu/fisheries/stock_enhancement/05_jfb529.pdf. July 17, 2004.

Scale Tales

1. John R. Paxton (1998). Paxton, J.R. & Eschmeyer, W.N.. ed. *Encyclopedia of Fishes*. San Diego: Academic Press. pp. 161–162.

2. Brian W. Coad and Don E. McAllister. "Dictionary of Ichthyology." http://www.briancoad.com/Dictionary/Complete%20Dictionary%20latest%20version.htm

While the Fish Was Swimming

1. "Shedd Aquarium: Australian Lungfish. http://www.sheddaquarium.org/australianlungfish.html; http://www.sheddaquarium.org/granddad.html

Croakin' Communications

1. Peter M. Narins. "Frog Communication." *Scientific American*. 1995. Reprinted here: http://www.acoustics.org/press/swa9501.html

2. Ibid.

How to Hear with No (External) Ears

1. Peter M. Narins, Gunther Ehret, and Jurgen Tautz. "Accessory Pathway for Sound Transfer in a Neotropical Frog." *Proc. Nati. Acad. Sci.* USA, Vol. 85, pp. 1508-1512, March 1988, Biophysics. http://www.ncbi.nlm.nih.gov/pmc/articles/PMC279801/pdf/pnas00257-0189.pdf

Frog Guts

1. David L. Haury. "Alternatives To Animal Dissection in School Science Classes" ERIC Clearinghouse for Science Mathematics and Environmental Education Columbus OH. ERIC Identifier: ED402155. Publication Date: 1996-09-00. http://www.ericdigests.org/1998-1/animal.htm

Salamander Crossing

1. U.S. Department of Transportation: Critter Crossing. http://www.fhwa.dot.gov/environment/wildlifecrossings/salamand.htm

Toad Abode

1. John McFarland "Drought Eases, Helping Endangered Toad." *The Austin-American Statesman*, October 14, 2009. http://www.statesman.com/news/content/news/stories/local/2009/10/14/1014toad.html?cxtype=rss&cxsvc=7&cxcat=52

Books

Arnosky, Jim. *Field Trips: Bug Hunting, Animal Tracking, Bird-watching, Shore Walking.* New York: HarperCollins, 2002.

Bakken, Aimee. *Uncover a Frog.* Charlotte, NC: Silver Dolphin Books, 2006.

Clark, Barry. *Amphibian* (DK Eyewitness Book). New York: DK Children, 2005.

Elliott, Lang. *The Frogs and Toads of North America: A Comprehensive Guide to Their Identification,Behavior, and Calls.* Boston: Mariner Books, 2009.

Mallory, Kenneth. *Swimming with Hammerhead Sharks.* New York: Houghton Mifflin Books for Children, 2001.

Miller, Sara Swan. *All Kinds of Eyes.* Tarrytown, NY: Marshall Cavendish Benchmark, 2008.

National Audubon Society. *National Audubon Society Field Guide to North American Fishes.* New York: Knopf, 2002.

Parker, Steve. *Fish* (DK Eyewitness Book). New York: DK Children, 2005.

Reebs, Stephan. *Fish Behavior in the Aquarium and in the Wild.* Ithaca, NY: Cornell University Press, 2001.

Turner, Pamela S. *The Frog Scientist.* New York: Houghton Mifflin Books for Children, 2009.

Works Consulted

"Animal Mummies." http://www.rmo.nl/english/current/exhibitions/archive/animal-mummies

Coad, Brian W., and Don E. McAllister. "Dictionary of Ichthyology." http://www.briancoad.com/Dictionary/Complete%20Dictionary%20latest%20version.htm

Eskandari, Armin. "Evolution of Fish." PPT Presentation: http://www.authorstream.com/Presentation/eskandari2000-103231-evolution-fish-part-1-systematic-armin-eskandari-fish1-science-technology-ppt-powerpoint/. Author: Armin Eskandari, Hydrobiology Division, Biology Deprtment, Faculty of Science, HACETTEPE University , Beytepe Kampus, 06800 , ANKARA, TURKEY, http://hacettepe.academia.edu/ArminEskandari.

Fairchild, E.A., and W.H.Howell "Factors Affecting the Post-release Survival of Cultured Juvenile *Pseudopleuronectes americanus.*" *Journal of Fish Biology.* 65 (Supplementary A): 69-87. http://cinemar.unh.edu/fisheries/stock_enhancement/05_jfb529.pdf. July 17, 2004.

Haury, David L. "Alternatives to Animal Dissection in School Science Classes." Columbus, OH: ERIC Clearinghouse for Science Mathematics and Environmental Education September 1996. http://www.ericdigests.org/1998-1/animal.htm

Kane, Daniel. "How Did Fins Evolve into Feet? Fossils Document Gradual Change in the Bones of Ancient Fish." *MSNBC Technology and Science.* Updated April 1, 2004. http://www.msnbc.msn.com/id/4638587/ns/technology_and_science-science/

Lewis, Joe. "Pond Ecology." Yale New Haven Teachers Institute. http://www.yale.edu/ynhti/curriculum/units/1992/5/92.05.07.x.html

Livingstone, Conway. "Was Rembrandt Stereoblind?" *The New England Journal of Medicine* (Sep 2004). 351 (12): 1264–5. doi:10.1056/NEJM200409163511224.

Marshall , Jessica. "Schooling Fish Inspire Efficient Wind Farms." *Discovery News.* November 30, 2009. http://news.discovery.com/earth/wind-farms-schooling-fish.html

McFarland, John. "Drought Eases, Helping Endangered Toad." October 14, 2009. *The Austin-American Statesman.* http://www.statesman.com/news/content/news/stories/local/2009/10/14/1014toad.html?cxtype=rss&cxsvc=7&cxcat=52

Narins, Peter M. "Frog Communication." *Scientific American*, 1995. Reprinted here: http://www.acoustics.org/press/swa9501.html

Narins, Peter M., Gunther Ehret, and Jurgen Tautz. "Accessory Pathway for Sound Transfer in a Neotropical Frog." *Proc. Nati. Acad. Sci. USA*, Vol. 85, pp. 1508–1512, March 1988, Biophysics. http://www.ncbi.nlm.nih.gov/pmc/articles/PMC279801/pdf/pnas00257-0189.pdf

Nelson, Joseph S. *Fishes of the World* (4th Edition). Hoboken, NJ: Wiley and Sons, 2006.

Orlans, F. Barbara, Tom L. Beauchamp, Rebecca Dresser, David B. Morton, and John P. Gluck. *The Human Use of Animals.* New York: Oxford University Press, 1998.

Paxton, J.R., and W.N. Eschmeyer, ed. *Encyclopedia of Fishes.* San Diego: Academic Press, 1998.

"Shedd Aquarium: Australian Lungfish http://www.sheddaquarium.org/australianlungfish.html

U.S. Department of Transportation: Critter Crossing. http://www.fhwa.dot.gov/environment/wildlifecrossings/salamand.htm

Wyman, Bruce, Ph.D., and L. Harold Stevenson, Ph.D. *The Facts on File Dictionary of Environmental Science* (Third Edition). New York: Infobase Publishing, 2007.

On the Internet

Aquarium Webcam Locator
http://www.webcamlocator.com/animals/aquarium_webcam_locator.htm

Discover Life: Salamander Identification Guide
http://pick4.pick.uga.edu/mp/20q?guide=Salamanders

Free, Downloadable Music Notation Paper
http://people.virginia.edu/~pdr4h/musicpaper/

Frog and Toad Identification and Sounds
http://www.naturesound.com/frogs/frogs.html

Frog Dissection Lab
http://www.ofsd.k12.wi.us/science/frogdiss.htm

New England Aquarium
http://www.neaq.org/index.php

Sounds of the Coqui
http://coquifrog.org/sounds_page.htm

amphibian (am-FIB-ee-an)—A vertebrate that is cold blooded, smooth skinned, and spends time in the water and on the land.

amphibious (am-FIB-ee-us)—Living on both land and in the water.

anadromous (an-ah-DROH-mus)—Living in saltwater but being born in and returning to freshwater to reproduce.

aquatic (ah-KWAH-tik)—Living in water.

binocular vision (bih-NOK-yoo-lur VIH-zhun)—Vision requiring two eyes.

caecilian (sih-SIL-yun)—Limbless amphibians that live chiefly in the tropics.

cartilaginous (kar-tih-LAH-jih-nus)—Having a skeleton made of cartilage (tough tissue) instead of bones.

crossopterygian (kros-op-tuh-RIH-jyan)—A type of fish that had paired lobes rather than fins.

depth perception (per-SEP-shun)—The ability to use a pair of eyes to judge distance.

Devonian (deh-VOH-nee-an) **period**—A period of time in earth's history, about 410 million years ago, when it is believed amphibians and bony fish began to develop.

dissect (dih-SEKT)—To cut apart or separate, usually to study an animal's anatomy.

ecosystem (EE-koh-sis-tem)—A community of plants and animals that live together.

ectotherm (EK-toh-therm)—A cold-blooded animal whose body temperature varies with the temperature around it.

endotherm (EN-doh-therm)—A warm-blooded animal whose body temperature stays constant without regard to the temperature around it.

fish—A vertebrate that is cold-blooded, has scales, breathes with gills, and lives in water.

flatfish—A fish with a compressed body, such as flounders, soles, and halibuts.

herbicide (ER-bih-syd)—A chemical used to kill unwanted plants.

ichthyologist (ik-thee-AH-luh-jist)—A fish scientist.

larva—A newly hatched, often wormlike form of a fish or insect before it starts changing into the adult form.

mammal—A warm-blooded vertebrate with fur or hair, including humans.

metabolism (meh-TAB-uh-lism)—The processes of eating and breathing for providing the body with energy.

monocular vision (muh-NAH-kyoo-lur VIH-zhun)—Vision requiring only one eye.

naturalist (NAT-chur-uh-list)—Someone who studies nature, including plants and animals.

nocturnal (nok-TUR-nul)—Being active at night.

otolith (AH-toh-lith)—A bone-like plate found in the ear of fish and other vertebrates.

siren—A type of land amphibian that resembles lizards.

synthesize (SIN-thuh-syz)—To create using electronic instruments.

terrestrial (ter-RES-tree-ul)—Living on land.

tympanum (tim-PAN-um)—A hard oval covering the hearing organs on either side of a frog's head.

vertebrate (VER-tuh-brit)—An animal that has a backbone.

viviparous (vih-VIH-par-us)—Giving birth to living offspring that develop within the body (as opposed to laying eggs).

ABOUT THE
AUTHOR

Carol Parenzan Smalley loves water. As a child, she swam competitively. (She loved to draft during swim practices!) As a teenager, she paddled canoes and kayaks through roaring rapids. As a young adult, she studied environmental engineering with the focus on water at Penn State. And, as an adult, she enjoys observing and photographing nature around her home in Adirondack Park in upstate New York. When not writing for young readers or playing in, on, or around water, she is a teaching artist in schools and libraries, where she conducts hands-on programs based on her books. To see where her next wet and wild adventure is taking her or to invite her to your school or library, visit her at www.CarolSmalley.com.